QUILTED
BAGS in a Weekend

QUILTED BAGS in a Weekend

25 purses, totes, and bags that you can make in no time

PHOTOGRAPHY BY TINO TEDALDI

Ellen Kharade

CREATIVE HOMEOWNER®, Upper Saddle River, New Jersey

First published in the US in 2005 by

CRE A TIVE
ARTS & CRAFTS™

An imprint of Creative Homeowner®,
Upper Saddle River, NJ

Creative Homeowner® is a registered trademark of
Federal Marketing Corporation

First published in 2005 by Cico Books Ltd
32 Great Sutton Street, London EC1V 0NB
Copyright © Cico Books 2004

Quilted Bags in a Weekend
Library of Congress card number: 2004113736

ISBN 1–58011–242–0

Illustrations by Kate Simunek
Edited by Alison Wormleighton
Photography by Tino Tedaldi
Designed by Christine Wood
Additional styling by Denise Brock
Additional makes by Emma Hardy and Hilary More

CREATIVE HOMEOWNER
A Division of Federal Marketing Corp.
24 Park Way
Upper Saddle River, NJ 07458
www.creativehomeowner.com

Printed and bound in China

contents

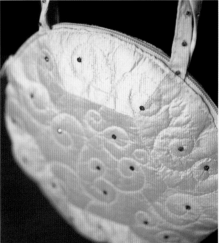

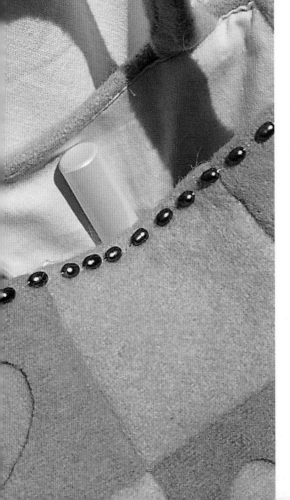

formal bags

A good selection of smart bags is an indispensable part of a wardrobe, particularly if they reflect your own personal style and favorite colors. There could be no better way to build up a truly individual collection of bags than to make them yourself, and patchwork offers a wealth of beautiful designs from which to choose. Using traditional techniques, you can create fresh, contemporary-looking bags in a wide range of fabrics. You will find a variety of styles in this chapter, ranging from the classic to the ultramodern. Although the techniques are quick and easy, the results are supremely stylish.

  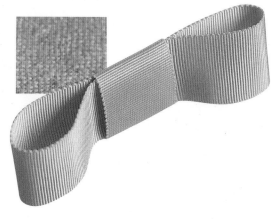

princess bag

This chic 1950s-inspired bag is made from squares of coordinating fabrics in shades of one color, to give it a fresh but distinctly sophisticated look. Grosgrain ribbon has been pleated to make a stylish trim around the top edge that matches the handles and simple bow. A glimpse of dark-color lining patterned with tiny polka-dots adds definition to the soft pastels.

The bag is 8¾ in. wide x 8 in. high (excluding handles) x 1¾ in. deep.

You will need:

◆ Scraps of four print fabrics in one color scheme, such as lime green

◆ ⅛ yd. of linen in a matching solid color

◆ Rotary cutter, acrylic ruler, cutting mat (optional)

◆ Matching sewing thread

◆ 10 x 20-in. piece of fusible interfacing

◆ ¼ yd. of print fabric in contrasting color, such as deep green polka dots, for lining

◆ 3⅛ yd. of 1-in. grosgrain ribbon

◆ Fade-away marker pen (optional)

Coordinating fabrics in lime green with grosgrain trim create a retro look.

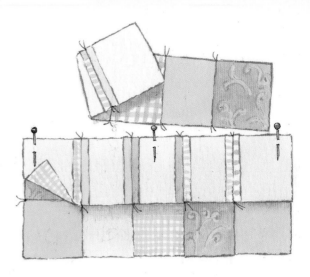

1 From the print fabrics and the linen, cut out forty 2¼-in. squares—about six to ten squares from each. A rotary cutter, acrylic ruler, and cutting mat are more accurate than scissors and will allow you to cut two layers of fabric at a time.

2 To piece the front and back, join five assorted solid and print squares into a row, right sides together and raw edges even, machine-stitching ¼-in. seams. Make seven more rows in the same way. Press all the seams open. Now pin two rows with right sides together and raw edges even, matching the seams; stitch a ¼-in. seam. Join two more rows to this section in the same way, to complete the front. Follow the same procedure to join the remaining four rows to make the back. Press the seams open.

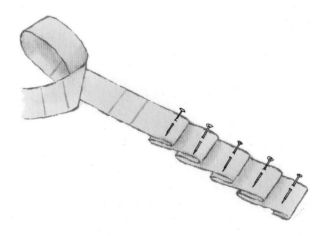

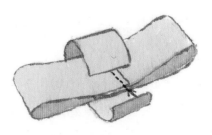

5 Using pins or a fade-away pen and starting at the left end of the ribbon, mark a line 1⅛ in. from the end and another line ½ in. further on. Now mark a third line a further 1⅛ in. along, followed by a fourth line another ½ in. along. Continue in the same way until you have marked 14 pairs of lines. Turn under the left end by ½ in., then pleat the ribbon by making an outer fold at the left line in each pair and an inner fold at the right line in each pair, pinning the pleats as you go. Check that the pleated ribbon is the right length to fit across the top of the bag exactly, and adjust the pleats as necessary. Cut the ribbon at the last mark, turning under ½ in. on the right end.

6 Repeat Step 5 to make a pleated ribbon for the back of the bag. Hand- or machine-baste the bottom edge of the pleated ribbons, removing the pins. Right sides together, pin and machine-baste the pleated ribbons to the top edge of the front and back on the right side, with the bottom edge of each ribbon even with the raw edge of the bag. For the bow, cut an 8½-in. length of ribbon, and overlap the ends by ¼ in. to form a loop, with the ends at the center. Machine-baste them together, through all three layers. Cut a 2½-in. length of ribbon, and wrap it over the center of the loop, overlapping the ends by ¼ in. Hand-sew the ends together, and then sew the ribbon to the loop.

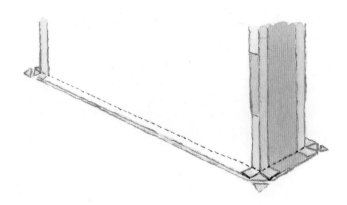

3 Cut two pieces of interfacing to the same size as the front and back (about 7½ x 9¼ in. each). Following the manufacturer's instructions, iron the interfacing to the wrong side of the patchwork front and back, making sure that the seam allowances are flat. From the linen, cut two pieces for the sides, each 2¼ in. wide and the same length as the height of the patchwork (about 7½ in.), and one piece for the base, 2¼ in. wide and the same length as the width of the patchwork (about 9¼ in.). From the lining fabric, cut pieces to the same size as the front, back, two sides, and base.

4 Right sides together and raw edges even, pin the sides to the front along the side edges, and machine-stitch ¼-in. seams, leaving the bottom ¼ in. of the seams unstitched. Join the remaining side edges of the sides to the back in the same way. Right sides together and raw edges even, pin the base to the bag using ¼-in. seams and allowing the unstitched portion of each side seam to open up at each corner, as shown. Adjust the size of the base or the width of the seams, if necessary, for a good fit. Machine-stitch, pivoting at the corners. Snip off the corners of the seam allowances, and press the seams open. Turn the bag right side out; press. Make the lining in the same way, but leave one long seam of the base unstitched.

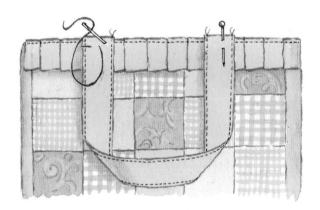

7 For the handles, cut two 24-in. lengths of ribbon and place one on top of the other. Pin and machine-stitch them together close to both side edges, then cut the length in half to make two double-thickness handles. Pin and hand-baste the ends of one handle to the right side of the front, on top of the pleated ribbon, 1¾ in. in from each side and with the ends even with the top edge of the bag. Pin and hand-baste the other handle to the back in the same way.

8 With the bag right side out and the lining wrong side out, slip the lining over the bag. With the top raw edges even and the side seams matching, pin the lining to the bag all the way around and machine-stitch a ¼-in. seam. Now pull the lining away from the bag, so it is right side out. Press the seam and press under ¼-in. seam allowances on the opening in the base of the lining. Slipstitch these edges together and push the lining inside the bag; press. Hand-sew the front side seam to the back side seam at the top of the bag, on the inside, as shown. Hand-sew the bow to the front of the bag near the top. Remove any visible basting.

 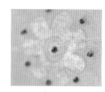 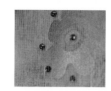

silk flower bag

This beautiful bag looks far more elaborate than it actually is. It features silk squares in different pale colors decorated with glass beads and hand-stamped gold flowers that are framed on the front with undecorated strips of silk in the same colors. In turn, the front is surrounded by sides, a back, a base, and strap handles in a deeper but similar shade of velvet. A satin lining provides a neat finish, and a button with a ribbon loop fastens the top.

 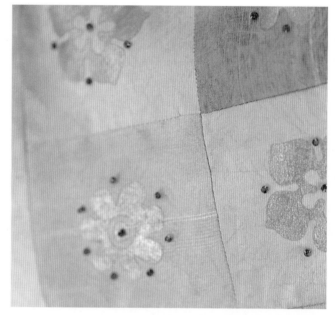

The bag is 9 in. wide x 9 in. high (excluding handles) x 1¾ in. deep.

You will need:

◆ ¼ yd. (in total) of silk in at least four colors, such as pale pink, mid pink, peach, and orange

◆ ⅓ yd. of velvet in a deeper tone, such as deep pink

◆ ⅓ yd. of satin fabric in same color as velvet, for lining

◆ Rotary cutter, acrylic ruler, cutting mat (optional)

◆ Piece of sponge, gold fabric paint, fine artist's paintbrush

◆ Flower stamps in two designs

◆ Matching sewing thread

◆ 10-in. square of fusible interfacing

◆ 30 small glass beads in a harmonizing color, such as lilac

◆ ¼ yd. of narrow ribbon in a harmonizing color, such as pink

◆ One button and one sequin in a color to match ribbon

Deep pink velvet sets off pale pink and peach silk stamped with gold.

1 From the silks, cut out two 3½-in. squares from each of two colors (or all four squares can be different colors), two 2¼ by 6½ in. strips from the third color, and two 2¼ x 10-in. strips from the fourth, all for the front. From the velvet, cut out a 10-in. square for the back and three 2¾ x 10-in. strips for the sides and base. From the satin, cut out two 10-in. squares and three 10 x 2¾-in. strips. A rotary cutter, acrylic ruler, and cutting mat are more accurate than scissors and will allow you to cut two layers of silk or satin at once. (The velvet should be cut one layer at a time.)

2 Place the pieces for the front on newspaper or a sheet of plastic to protect your work surface. Dip the piece of sponge in a little of the paint, and then lightly dab the paint onto one of the stamps. Press the stamp onto the center of one silk square, and carefully lift it away. Use a fine paint-brush and a little more paint to touch up any areas that look thin. Use the same stamp for the diagonally opposite patch, and the second stamp for the other two silk patches. Let it dry. Place a clean cloth over the motif and iron to fix the design, following the paint manufacturer's instructions.

5 If desired, make a small dart in each side at the top, to give the bag some shape. Press under ½ in. all around the top edge of the bag.

6 For the handles, cut two 1½ x 20-in. strips of velvet. Fold one long edge of one strip into the center, wrong sides together, and hand-baste in place. Repeat for the other long edge of the strip. Turn in ¼ in. at each end, and then fold the strip in half lengthwise, enclosing all the raw edges. Pin and machine-stitch along the long edge and both ends. Make the second handle in the same way. Pin and hand-baste the ends of one handle to the wrong side of the front, and the ends of the other to the wrong side of the back, positioning all four ends the same distance from the sides.

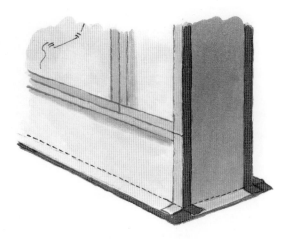

3 To piece the front, pin and machine-stitch the pieces, right sides together and raw edges even, using ¼-in. seams and pressing the seams open as you go, working in the following sequence: join the top two silk squares, do the same for the bottom two silk squares, then stitch these two sections together, matching the seams. Stitch one of the shorter silk strips to each side, and then the two longer silk strips to the top and bottom. From the interfacing, cut out a 10-in. square. Following the manufacturer's instructions, iron the interfacing to the wrong side of the patchwork, making sure that the seam allowances are flat. Decorate the stamped flowers by hand-sewing glass beads to the centers and around the edges.

4 Right sides together and raw edges even, pin the long edges of the two velvet strips for the sides to the side edges of the front. Machine-stitch ½-in. seams, leaving the bottom ½ in. of the seams unstitched. Join the remaining long edges of the sides to the side edges of the velvet back in the same way. Right sides together and raw edges even, pin the base to the bag, using ½-in. seams and allowing the unstitched portion of each side seam to open up at each corner, as shown. Adjust the size of the base or the width of the seams, if necessary, for a good fit. Machine-stitch, pivoting at the corners. Snip off the corners of the seam allowances, and press the seams open.

7 Make the lining from the satin pieces in the same way as for the bag, Steps 4 and 5. Turn the bag right side out. With the lining wrong side out, push it into the bag, matching the side seams. Carefully pin the lining to the bag around the top. Machine-stitch close to the edge, catching in the carriers and tab at the same time. Remove the basting. To give the handles extra strength, stitch again parallel to the previous stitching, being sure to stitch over the ends of the handles.

8 Make a loop with the narrow ribbon and hand-sew it to the wrong side of the back at the center. Sew a button to the right side of the front, embellishing it with a sequin sewn to its center, and then secure the bag by looping the ribbon over the button.

modern black and white bag

Made from random-width patches of black-and-white prints, this stylish bag goes equally well with white sportswear or black evening wear, as well as with stripes or solid colors, such as red. The round black handles echo both the shape of the bag and the color theme, while the diagonal arrangement of the patches adds to the dynamic feel. All the sewing is quick and easy, because the patches, which are all rectangles of the same length, are simply sewn together into long strips, which are joined without the need for any seam matching.

The bag is 14½ in. in diameter (excluding handles).

You will need:

- ⅛ yd. each of six fabrics in black-and-white prints
- ¼ yd. of black fabric
- Rotary cutter, acrylic ruler, cutting mat (optional)
- Matching sewing thread
- ½ yd. of fusible interfacing

- Paper for pattern
- 12-in. length of string
- Pair of 6-in.-wide round black handles
- 16 round pearl buttons
- ½ yd. of white or black fabric, for lining

Restricting the bag's colors to black and white creates an ultramodern look.

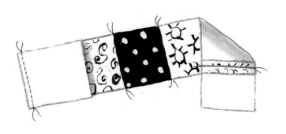

1 From each of the seven fabrics, cut a strip 3½ in. wide and about 1 yd. long. Now cut the strips into pieces varying from about 1½ in. to 4 in. wide, to make about 80 pieces that are all the same length but are different widths. (The solid-black pieces will look best if they are no more than about 2 in. wide.) A rotary cutter, acrylic ruler, and cutting mat are more accurate than scissors and will allow you to cut two layers of fabric at a time.

2 Pin one piece to a second one in a different fabric along one side edge, right sides together and raw edges even, and machine-stitch a ¼-in. seam. Repeat to join more pieces together until you have a row of about seven to nine pieces, with a total width of at least 15½ in., and including a variety of fabrics and widths. Make nine more rows in the same way. Press the seams open.

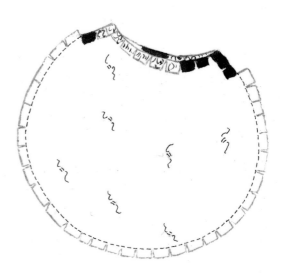

5 Place one pieced section so the corner is at the top, like a diamond, and the rows of patches are on the diagonal. Pin the pattern to it with the cutout curve at the top. Make sure the fabric extends up to or beyond the edge of the pattern all the way around. Cut out the pieced shape. Repeat for the other patchwork square. Hand-sew buttons to the patchwork seamlines in a regular pattern.

6 Right sides together and raw edges even, pin the two pieced sections together so the cutout areas are on top of each other. Machine-stitch a ½-in. seam around the edge, leaving the curved top unstitched. Clip into the seam allowances of the seam, and press it open. Press under ½ in. on the top edges, clipping into the seam allowances. Using the pattern, cut out two pieces of the lining fabric, and make the lining in the same way. Turn the bag right side out, and press.

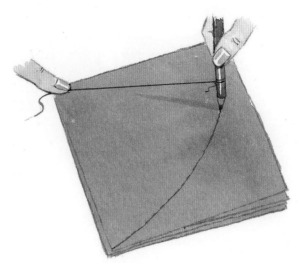

3 Right sides together and raw edges even, pin one row to another, trying to avoid placing pieces from the same fabric next to each other. Machine-stitch a ¼-in. seam. Now join three more rows to this section in the same way, so that the pieced section is roughly square and the light and dark tones are fairly balanced. It doesn't matter if the ends of the rows are not quite even. Join the remaining five rows in the same way to form another square. Press the seams open. Cut out two squares of fusible interfacing the same size as each pieced section. Following the manufacturer's instructions, iron the interfacing to the wrong side of each section, making sure that the seam allowances are flat.

4 To make a circular paper pattern, cut out a square of paper exactly the same size as the patchwork section at its narrowest point (about 15½ in. across). Fold the paper in fourths. Tie one end of the string to a pencil, and hold the other end at the folded corner of the square (the center when it is unfolded) so you can use them like a compass. Adjust the string until the pencil reaches to the edge of the paper with the string taut, then draw a quarter-circle. Cut this out and unfold it—the pattern should be a circle with a diameter of 16 in. Using one handle as a guide, cut a shallow arc out of the edge of the pattern.

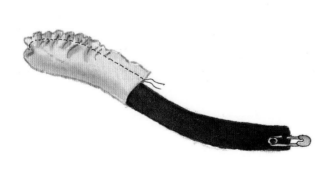

7 For the carriers, cut out a 2¼ x 21-in. strip from the black fabric. Fold it in half lengthwise, right sides together, and then pin and machine-stitch a ¼-in. seam down the long edge. Attach a safety pin to one end. Thread the safety pin through the tube of fabric, pulling it through to turn the fabric right side out. Press it flat, and then cut it into six 3½-in. carriers.

8 Wrap one carrier over one handle, and hand-baste the ends together. Repeat for two more carriers. Pin the ends of one to the inside of the front at the top, 1 in. from the side seam. Pin another carrier 1 in. from the other side, and a third in the center. Wrap the remaining three over the second handle; hand-baste; and pin in the same positions on the back. Machine-baste all six carriers. With the lining wrong side out, push it into the bag, matching the side seams, and pin it around the top. Machine-stitch close to the edge, catching in the carriers at the same time. Remove the basting.

pyramid bag

Three floral prints and a plaid, all in harmonizing colors, are used for the pieces making up this striking bag. Rectangles of the same width, but of random lengths, are sewn together into strips. The sides of the strips are then cut at angles before being stitched together, creating the bag's tapered shape. At the top, a solid-color band, trimmed with a matching ribbon and discreetly decorated with small pearl buttons, provides a crisp finish to the patchwork, complemented by the curve of the handles.

The bag is about 12 in. wide x 13 in. high (excluding handles).

You will need:

- ¼ yd. each of three print fabrics and ½ yd. of a fourth print, all in coordinating colors
- Rotary cutter, acrylic ruler, cutting mat (optional)
- Matching sewing thread
- Paper for patterns
- ⅛ yd. of fabric in a solid color to match others

- 1 yd. of ½-in.-wide matching velvet ribbon
- ½ yd. of fusible interfacing
- ½ yd. of ¾-in.-wide matching satin ribbon
- Pair of 6-in.-wide curved handles
- Snap fastener
- 10 round pearl buttons

Tortoiseshell-effect handles set off a burgundy color theme.

1 From each of the four print fabrics, cut a strip 4¼ in. wide and about 1 yd. long. Now cut the strips into pieces varying from about 1½ in. to 3½ in. long, to make about 50 pieces that are all the same width but are different lengths. A rotary cutter, acrylic ruler, and cutting mat are more accurate than scissors and will allow you to cut two layers of fabric at a time.

2 Pin the bottom edge of one piece to the top edge of a piece in a different fabric, right sides together and raw edges even, and machine-stitch a ¼-in. seam. Repeat to join more pieces together until you have a vertical row of about five to seven patches, with a total length of 12½ in., and including a variety of fabrics and sizes. Make seven more vertical rows in the same way. Press the seams open.

5 Cut two strips of solid-color fabric 2¼ in. wide and as long as the width of the top edge of the front (about 8½ in.). Right sides together and raw edges even, pin the long edge of one strip to the top edge of the front; machine-stitch a ¼-in. seam. Join the other strip to the back in the same way. Pin and topstitch velvet ribbon to the strip about ¼ in. above the lower edge of the strip, on both the front and back. Cut two pieces of interfacing and two pieces of the fourth fabric for the lining, all to the same size as the front and back. Following the manufacturer's instructions, iron the interfacing to the wrong side of the patchwork front and back, making sure that the seam allowances are flat.

6 Pin the front to the back, right sides together and raw edges even, and machine-stitch a ½-in. seam around the sides and bottom, pivoting at the bottom corners. Snip off the corners of the seam allowances and press open the seams. Press under a ½-in. hem along the top raw edges. Make the lining from the two lining pieces in the same way.

3 To make the two patterns, cut a paper rectangle 7¼ in. wide x 12½ in. long. At the top, mark points 3 in. from the left edge and 2¼ in. from the right edge. At the bottom, mark a point 3 in. from the right edge. Draw a straight line between the left-hand mark at the top and the mark at the bottom. Draw a second line between the right-hand mark at the top and the bottom right corner. Now cut along both these lines and discard the triangle on the right.

4 Decide where each vertical row will be positioned on the front and back, and, starting from the left, label the front vertical rows 1 to 4 and the back ones (again starting from the left) 5 to 8. Pin the wider pattern to the right side of row 3 and cut out the shape. Repeat for row 7, then turn the pattern over and use it to cut out rows 2 and 6. With the other pattern, cut out rows 4 and 8, then turn it over and cut out rows 1 and 5. Now join the four rows of the front in the correct order, pinning and machine-stitching the pieces, right sides together and raw edges even, using ¼-in. seams. Repeat for the back. Press the seams open.

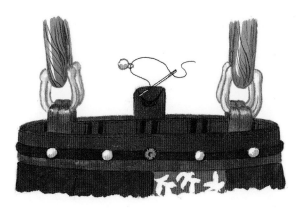

7 For the handle carriers, cut four 2-in. lengths of satin ribbon, and thread these through the rings at the ends of the handles. Baste the ends together. Using the handles as a guide to positioning, pin and then baste these carriers to the top edge of the bag front and back, on the wrong side. For the tab, cut two 1¾ x 2½-in. rectangles from one of the patterned fabrics. Pin one to the other around the edges, right sides together and raw edges even. Stitch a ¼-in. seam down each side, tapering to a point at one end. Snip off the corners of the seam allowances at the bottom. Turn right side out and press. Pin and baste the tab to the top edge of the bag back, centering it on the wrong side.

8 Turn the bag right side out. With the lining wrong side out, push it into the bag, matching the side seams. Carefully pin the lining to the bag around the top. Machine-stitch close to the edge, catching in the carriers and the tab at the same time. Remove the basting. Hand-sew the "ball" of the snap to the underside of the tab and the "socket" of the snap to the right side of the bag near the top, so that they align exactly. Hand-sew the buttons to the ribbon on the front and back, and sew one to the outside of the tab so it is in line with those on the ribbon.

checkerboard heart bag

Heart motifs decorate the checkerboard-pattern front of this stylish bag made from felted wool. The curvy lines of the hearts contrast with the straight lines of the grid pattern, while the muted colors in combination with the sensible, sturdy shape and upstanding handles provide a sophisticated counterbalance to the folk-art motifs. A row of dark seed pearls adds definition. Inside the bag, the lining has a useful pocket, which is decorated with glass beads.

The bag is 9½ in. wide x 7½ in. high (excluding handles) x 3½ in. deep.

You will need:

◆ Paper and stiff cardstock for patterns

◆ ⅓ yd. (total) of felted wool in three similar colors, such as green, turquoise, and blue

◆ ⅓ yd. of cotton fabric in a coordinating color, such as pale blue, for lining

◆ Matching sewing thread

◆ Fine-point marker pen and fabric glue

◆ 5 x 32-in. piece of artist's plastic mesh (available from craft stores)

◆ 18 glass beads and 22 seed pearls or sequins

Cool, harmonious colors lend elegance to a lighthearted design.

1 Enlarge and transfer the templates from page 120 onto paper, then cut out the patterns. From the first color, cut out one back using the pattern, one 5 x 10¾-in. rectangle for the base, and one 2 x 31½-in. strip for handles. From the second color, cut out two sides using the pattern. From all three colors, use the patterns to cut out the nine pieces for the front, making sure that adjacent pieces are not in the same color and that the central and corner pieces are not in the first color. From the lining fabric, cut out two pieces from the back pattern (one will be used for the lining front), two sides using the side pattern, and a 5 x 10¾-in. base.

2 Use the heart template to make a pattern from cardstock. With the marker pen, draw around the heart pattern on the center and corner pieces for the front, placing the pattern in the center of each. Using very sharp scissors, carefully cut out the shapes. Seal the edges of the hearts with fabric glue on the wrong side and allow to dry.

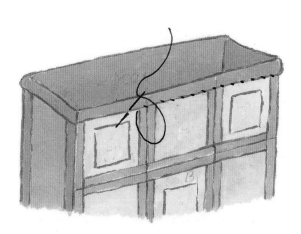

5 Press under ¼ in. all around the top edge of the bag, hand-sew neatly in place, and then turn the bag right side out. Cut out two strips of plastic mesh, one measuring 4½ x 10¼ in. and the other ¾ x 31½ in., and place the shorter one in the bottom of the bag, hand-sewing the corners to the inside of the bag.

6 Press under ¼ inch on the long edges of the long fabric strip. Wrap the strip around the long mesh strip, right side out, and slipstitch the folded edges together. Cut the fabric-enclosed mesh in half, and hand-sew the ends of one of these handles to the wrong side of the front, and the ends of the other to the wrong side of the back, positioning all four ends the same distance from the sides.

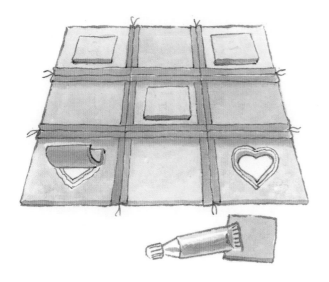

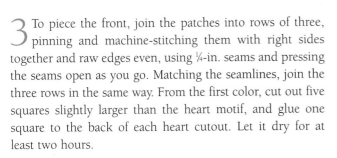

3 To piece the front, join the patches into rows of three, pinning and machine-stitching them with right sides together and raw edges even, using ¼-in. seams and pressing the seams open as you go. Matching the seamlines, join the three rows in the same way. From the first color, cut out five squares slightly larger than the heart motif, and glue one square to the back of each heart cutout. Let it dry for at least two hours.

4 Right sides together and raw edges even, pin the sides to the front along the side edges and machine-stitch ¼-in. seams, leaving the bottom ¼ in. of the seams unstitched. Join the remaining side edges of the sides to the back in the same way. Right sides together and raw edges even, pin the base to the bag using ¼-in. seams and allowing the unstitched portion of each side seam to open up at each corner, as shown. Adjust the size of the base or the width of the seams, if necessary, for a good fit. Machine-stitch, pivoting at the corners. Snip off the corners of the seam allowances, and press the seams open.

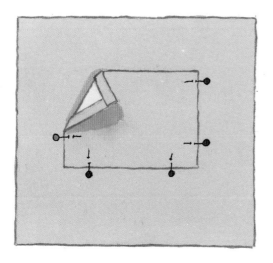

7 From the lining fabric, cut out a 4 x 5-in. rectangle for a pocket. Press under ½ in. on all four edges, and topstitch one long edge. With this edge at the top, pin the pocket to the right side of the lining back, 1¾ in. from the top. Topstitch the pocket down one side, along the bottom, and up the other side. Also topstitch vertically down the center. Decorate the edges of the pocket with a row of beads

8 Make up the lining as in Step 4, then press under ¼ in. around the top edge. With the lining wrong side out, push the lining inside the bag, matching the side seams. Pin the lining to the bag around the top. Machine-stitch close to the edge, catching in the handles at the same time. Hand-sew seed pearls or sequins along the top of the bag at the front.

yo-yo bag

Fabric circles gathered up to form rosettes, known as yo-yos among quilters, create a delightful three-dimensional effect on this bag. Sewn together and then to the central panel, they are very quick to make. The use of plaids for the yo-yos on the bag was inspired by Scottish tam-o'-shanters, but checked or striped fabrics would work particularly well, too. With lighter-colored fabrics you could embroider cross stitches or French knots on each yo-yo. Inside the bag is a handy pocket.

The bag is 11¼ in. wide x 9¼ in. high (excluding handles) x 1¾ in. deep.

You will need:

◆ Compass and paper for pattern

◆ ¼ yd. each of non-bulky fabric such as cotton in three coordinating plaids

◆ Matching quilting thread and sewing thread

◆ ¼ yd. of a fabric in a coordinating solid color, such as peach

◆ ½ yd. of a fabric in a second coordinating solid color, such as green

◆ Rotary cutter, acrylic ruler, cutting mat (optional)

◆ ⅓ yd. of fusible interfacing

◆ 2 x 12-in. piece of artist's plastic mesh (available from craft stores)

A single small pattern in coordinating colors is best for the yo-yos on this bag.

1 Using a compass, draw a circle with a diameter of 3¾ in. on a piece of paper, and cut it out. Use this pattern to cut out eight circles from each of the three plaid fabrics. Turn under ¼ in. around the edge of each circle, and finger-press. Knot a piece of quilting thread, and hand-sew even running stitches all around the hemmed edge of one circle, overlapping the first and last stitches. Pull the ends to gather up the fabric tightly. Make several backstitches to secure the thread before cutting it. Do the same for the other 23 circles.

2 With the hole in the center of each yo-yo, press them gently beneath a damp towel, using a steam iron. Place two yo-yos together with the holes facing outward, and join them with several hand-stitches at one edge. Continue sewing them together until you have six rows of four yo-yos each. Now sew three rows together in the same way, with several hand-stitches joining adjacent yo-yos; these will go on the front of the bag. Repeat to sew three more rows together, for the back of the bag.

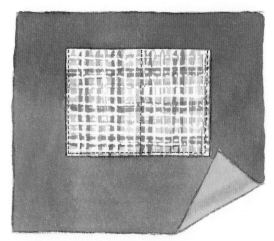

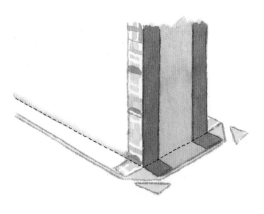

5 From the other solid-color fabric, cut three 10¼ x 12¼-in. rectangles (for the back and the lining front and back), four 2¾ x 10¼-in. strips (for the sides and the lining sides), two 2¾ x 12¼-in. strips (for the base and the lining base), and two 3 x 16-in. strips (for the handles). If you would like a pocket inside the bag, also cut a 5½ x 7½-in. rectangle from the third plaid fabric, press under ¼ in. on each edge, and stitch across one long edge. Pin the pocket centrally to one lining piece. Topstitch along the side and bottom edges and also from the top edge to the bottom edge of the pocket to create two compartments.

6 Right sides together and raw edges even, pin the bag sides to the bag front along the side edges, and machine-stitch ½-in. seams, leaving the bottom ½ in. of the seams unstitched. Join the remaining side edges of the sides to the bag back in the same way. Right sides together and raw edges even, pin the base to the bag using ½-in. seams and allowing the unstitched portion of each side seam to open up at each corner, as shown. Adjust the size of the base or the width of the seams, if necessary, for a good fit. Machine-stitch, pivoting at the corners. Snip off the corners of the seam allowances, and press the seams open. Press under ½ in. around the top edge. Make the lining in the same way.

3 From one solid-color fabric, cut two 5¾ x 7¾-in. rectangles. From the third plaid fabric, cut four 2¾ x 5¾-in. strips and four 2¾ x 12¼-in. strips. A rotary cutter, acrylic ruler, and cutting mat are more accurate than scissors and will allow you to cut two layers of fabric at a time. Right sides together and raw edges even, pin a short plaid strip to each short edge of the solid-color rectangle. Machine-stitch ¼-in. seams. Press the seams open. Now join a long strip to the top and another to the bottom of the rectangle in the same way. Repeat for the remaining pieces.

4 Cut out two 10¼ x 12¼-in. rectangles of fusible inter-facing. Following the manufacturer's instructions, iron the interfacing to the wrong side of each pieced section, making sure that the seam allowances are flat. Hand-sew the yo-yos to the center rectangle of each pieced section using a few tiny stitches at the edge of each yo-yo.

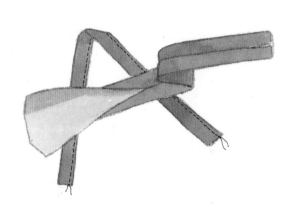

7 Cut a 1¾ x 11¼-in. rectangle of plastic mesh (adjusting the size to fit the base if you adjusted that in Step 6). Hand-sew it to the wrong side of the base using a few stitches at each side. For the handles, fold one long edge of one strip into the center, wrong sides together. Repeat for the other long edge of the strip, and then fold the strip in half lengthwise, enclosing the raw edges. Press. Pin and machine-stitch along the long edge. Make the second handle in the same way. Pin and hand-baste the ends of one handle to the wrong side of the front, and the ends of the other handle to the wrong side of the back. The center of each end should be in line with the edge of the central rectangle on the front and back.

8 Turn the bag right side out, and press. With the lining wrong side out, push it into the bag, matching the side seams. Carefully pin the lining to the bag around the top. Machine-stitch close to the edge, catching in the ends of the handles at the same time. Remove the basting.

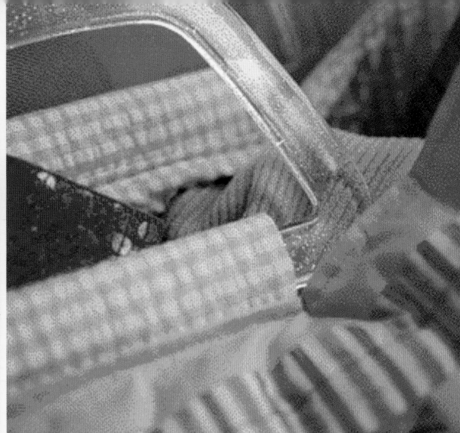

shoppers and totes

Totes are the most hard-working of all types of bags, but the beautiful patchwork designs in this chapter prove that they can also be fashionable. Whether you want an elegant silk and velvet tote, a cheerful carryall in bright pastel cottons with bamboo handles, a girl's overnight bag, or a variety of stylish totes in geometric prints, there are plenty of inspiring projects from which to choose. Ranging from the compact to the spacious, they will prove ideal traveling companions for anything from a trip to the grocery store to a day at the beach.

flower and striped tote

A bold, modern floral fabric is teamed with a coordinating stripe to great effect to make this contemporary-looking patchwork tote. Use solid colors alongside the prints so that the pattern does not overpower the style. To make a handy, practical bag suitable for everyday use, line it with batting for protection and strength. Here, the layers are joined together with simple ditch-quilting, where stitching along the patchwork seams holds the structure in place.

The tote is 22 in. wide x 14 in. high (excluding handles).

You will need:

◆ ¼ yd. each of floral print and striped fabric

◆ 1⅛ yd. (in total) of two solid-color fabrics

◆ Rotary cutter, acrylic ruler, cutting mat (optional)

◆ Matching sewing thread

◆ ⅔ yd. of lightweight polyester batting

Flowers and stripes make a perfect summer style combination.

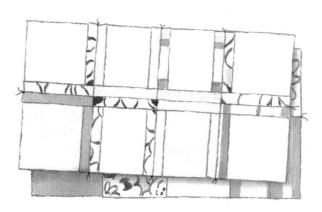

1 For the front, cut out eight 6-in. squares of different fabrics, such as three floral, two striped, and three solid-color. A rotary cutter, acrylic ruler, and cutting mat are more accurate than scissors and will allow you to cut two layers of fabric at a time. Arrange the pieces in a pleasing pattern. Right sides together and raw edges even, pin the top four squares together in a row. Machine-stitch ¼-in. seams and press the seams open. Repeat for the bottom row of squares.

2 Right sides together and raw edges even, pin the two rows together, matching the seams, to make a panel of eight squares. Machine-stitch ¼-in. seams; press the seams open. Repeat Steps 1 and 2 to make the back of the bag.

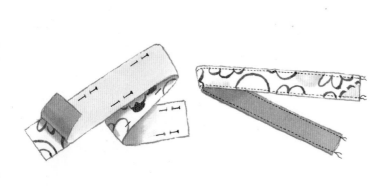

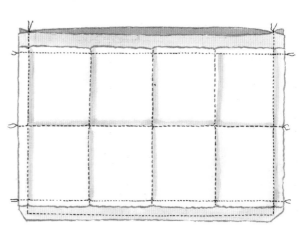

5 For the straps, cut four 1½ x 25-in. strips of fabric, two in floral and two in solid-color fabric. Right sides together, pin a floral strip to a solid strip along the long edges and machine-stitch ¼-in. seams. Turn the strap right side out by fastening a safety pin to a layer of fabric at one end of the strap and threading it through to the other end. Press the strap flat and topstitch along each long edge. Repeat to make a second strap from the other two strips of fabric.

6 Right sides together and raw edges even, pin the front and back pieces together along the side and bottom edges. Machine-stitch a ¼-in. seam, pivoting at the corners. Snip off the corners of the seam allowance at the bottom, turn the bag right side out, and press. For the lining, cut two 14¾ x 22½-in. pieces of solid-colored fabric. Right sides together and raw edges even, pin and machine-stitch a ¼-in. seam along each short edge. Press the seams open.

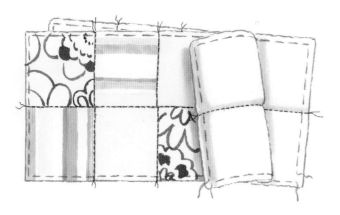

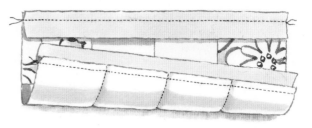

3 Cut two pieces of batting to the same size as the front and back (about 11½ x 22½ in.). Lay a patchwork panel over one piece, and pin and baste the two layers together. Repeat with the other patchwork panel and the second piece of batting. Now "ditch-quilt" the layers by machine-stitching over the seams. Repeat with the other patchwork panel and the second piece of batting. Remove the basting.

4 Cut four 2 x 22½-in. solid-color strips for the top and bottom edging of the front and back. Pin one strip along the top edge of one patchwork panel, and one strip along the bottom of the panel; machine-stitch ¼-in. seams. Press open the seams. Repeat for the second patchwork panel and the remaining strips.

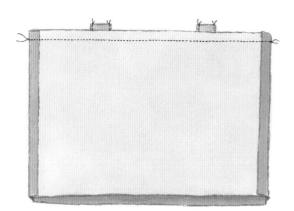

7 Right sides together, pull the lining over the bag, with the raw edges even at the top. Place one handle on the front of the bag, sandwiched between the patchwork and lining, with the ends ¼ inch above the raw edge of the bag; the outside edges of the handle should be aligned with the seamline between the two outer pieces (see photo). Baste the ends in place. Repeat for the other handle. Pin the lining to the bag around the top, and machine-stitch a ¼-in. seam all the way around. Turn the lining right side out, press under ¼ in. on the raw edges, and slipstitch them together. Push the lining inside the bag, and press. Remove any visible basting.

summertime tote

Fresh colors and simple patterns are ideal for this cheerful tote that features the ever-popular patchwork design known as flying geese. A small sprigged cotton is used for the five triangles that make up each block on the front, with a matching gingham for the smaller triangles framing the larger ones. Narrow sashing strips in the same sprigged print separate the three flying-geese blocks, while a polka-dot cotton surrounds them. The back is quick and easy to make up, simply comprising rectangles in the three fabrics. The handles are made from strips of the sprigged print.

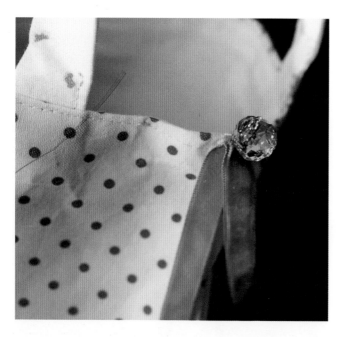
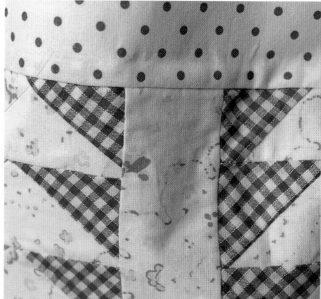

The bag is 15½ in. wide x 17 in. high (excluding handles).

You will need:

◆ ½ yd. of a print fabric in a summery color such as sky blue and white

◆ Rotary cutter, acrylic ruler, cutting mat (optional)

◆ ⅓ yd. of a small-check gingham in the same color

◆ ½ yd. of a polka-dot fabric in the same color

◆ Matching sewing thread

◆ Paper for pattern

◆ ½ yd. of fusible interfacing

◆ ½ yd. of white fabric, for lining

◆ ⅔ yd. of narrow ribbon in the same color as print fabric

◆ Two large glass beads

Sky blue is the perfect color for a bag with a flying-geese design.

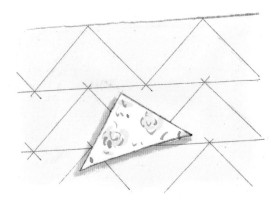

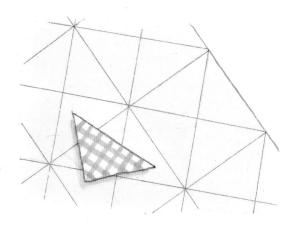

1 On the wrong side of the print fabric, draw lines 2¼ in. apart on the straight grain until you have marked out strips totaling about 2 yd. in length. On alternate lines mark a point 2¼ in. from one edge and then further points 4½ in. apart. On the remaining lines, mark the first point 4½ in. from the edge and other points 4½ in. apart. Draw straight lines between the points in a zigzag pattern and then cut along the lines, until you have 15 triangles. A rotary cutter, acrylic ruler, and cutting mat are more accurate than scissors and will allow you to cut two layers of fabric at a time.

2 On the wrong side of the gingham, draw a grid of lines 2½ in. apart on the bias (diagonal), until you have marked out about 15 squares. Now draw a zigzag pattern connecting alternate points on adjacent lines. Cut along the lines, to make 30 smaller triangles. Right sides together and raw edges even, pin the long edge of one small triangle to one of the short edges of a large triangle, and machine-stitch a ¼-in. seam. Join a second small triangle to the other short edge of the large triangle in the same way, forming a rectangle. Repeat until you have 15 rectangles. Press the seams open and trim off the corners of the seam allowances, even with the raw edges.

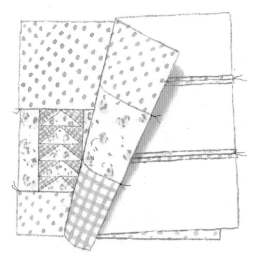

5 From the polka-dot fabric, cut two rectangles to the width of the pieced section (about 16½ in.), the first one 7½ in. deep and the other 3 in. deep. Pin the first to the top of the pieced section and the second to the bottom along the long edges, right sides together and raw edges even. Stitch ¼-in. seams. This will be the front. For the back, cut three rectangles to the same width as the front. The first, from the polka-dot fabric, should be 5 in. deep and the second, from the print, 7 in. deep. The third, from the gingham should be equal to the depth of the front less 11 in. (or about 7 in.). Join these in the same way as for the front.

6 Enlarge and transfer the template from page 121 onto paper, then cut out the pattern. For the front of the bag, pin the pattern to the center of the pieced section and cut out the shape. Repeat for the back. Also use the pattern to cut out two pieces of fusible interfacing and two pieces of lining fabric. Following the manufacturer's instructions, iron the interfacing to the wrong side of the front and back, making sure that the seam allowances are flat. Right sides together and raw edges even, pin the front to the back around the sides and bottom. Machine-stitch a ½-in. seam. Clip into the seam allowances on the curves. Press the seam open and press under a ½-in. hem along the top raw edges. Make the lining from the two lining pieces in the same way.

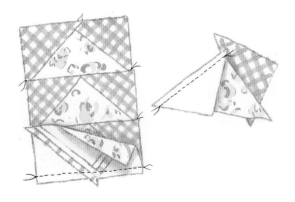

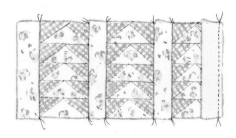

3 Right sides together and raw edges even, pin the bottom edge of one pieced rectangle to the top edge of another, being careful to stitch just through the point of the triangle. Machine-stitch a ¼-in. seam. Join three more pieced rectangles to these two in the same way. Now stitch five more pieced rectangles together in the same way, and then join the last five, so that you have three vertical rows in all. Press the seams open.

4 From the print fabric, cut four strips 2 in. wide and as long as the height of the pieced sections (about 8½ in.). Join the long edges of the strips to those of the pieced sections, right sides together and raw edges even, with the strips and vertical rows alternating. Machine-stitch ¼-in. seams, being careful to stitch through the point of each triangle. Press the seams open.

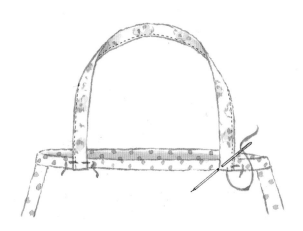

7 For the handles, cut two 3 x 16-in. strips of the print fabric. Fold one long edge of one strip into the center, wrong sides together. Repeat for the other long edge of the strip, and then fold the strip in half lengthwise, enclosing the raw edges. Press. Pin and machine-stitch along the long edge. Make the second handle in the same way. Pin and hand-baste the ends of one handle to the wrong side of the front and the ends of the other to the wrong side of the back, positioning the center of each 2 in. from the sides.

8 Turn the bag right side out and press. With the lining wrong side out, push it into the bag, matching the side seams. Carefully pin the lining to the bag around the top. Machine-stitch close to the edge, catching in the ends of the handles at the same time. Remove the basting. Cut two 11-in. lengths of ribbon, and hand-sew the center of each to the top edge of the bag at the side seam. Hand-sew a bead on top of each ribbon.

silk and velvet tote

Subtly different tones of one color allow the eye to focus on the pattern and texture of this beautiful tote. On both the front and the back, strips and squares of solid-color silk and velvet contrast with squares cut from fabrics in several small-scale patterns, while velvet straps add rich texture. The bag is flat, with the back and front simply stitched together, but a shaped outline and a patterned lining add interest. A line of matching buttons at front and back adds further subtle detail.

The bag is 22 in. wide x 15¼ in. high (excluding handles).

You will need:

◆ Scraps of four print fabrics, all in the same color scheme, such as purple

◆ ½ yd. each of solid-colored silk and velvet in same color as prints

◆ Rotary cutter, acrylic ruler, cutting mat (optional)

◆ Matching sewing thread

◆ Paper for pattern

◆ 1½ yd. of fusible interfacing

◆ Ten buttons

◆ ⅔ yd. of print fabric, for lining

Silks and velvets mix with delicate patterns in shades of purple.

1 From the prints and the silk and velvet, cut out twenty-four 4-in. squares. From the silk cut out four 4 x 21½-in. strips. A rotary cutter, acrylic ruler, and cutting mat are more accurate than scissors and will allow you to cut two layers of silk at once. (The velvet should be cut one layer at a time.)

2 To piece the front and back, join six assorted silk, velvet, and print squares into a row, right sides together and raw edges even, using ¼-in. seams. Make three more rows in the same way, and then press all the seams open. For the front, join one of these rows to a silk strip along the long edges, right sides together and raw edges even, using ¼-in. seams. Repeat for another silk strip and another row of squares, then join the two sections in the same way, with the silk strips and the rows of squares alternating. Press the seams open. For the back, join the remaining two silk strips and two rows of squares in the same way as for the front.

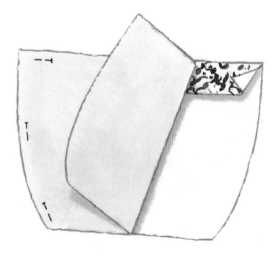

5 Turn the bag right side out. Sew five buttons onto the upper silk strip at the front, and do the same for the back, lining them up with the seams joining the squares.

6 At the top of the length of lining fabric, fold under 2½ in., and then pin the pattern to the lining fabric so that the top edge of the pattern is on the fold. Cut it out, then repeat to make a second lining piece. Unfold the tops of the lining pieces and, right sides together, stitch the two pieces together as in Step 4.

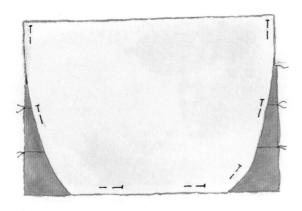

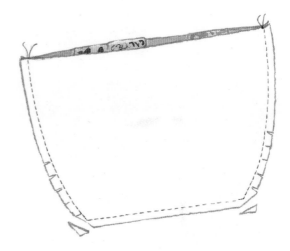

3 Enlarge and transfer the template from page 122 onto paper, and then cut out the pattern. Center and pin the pattern to the patchwork for the front and back pieces. Cut out both pieces.

4 Use the same pattern to cut out two pieces of fusible interfacing. Following the manufacturer's instructions, iron the interfacing to the wrong side of the patchwork front and back, making sure that the seam allowances are lying flat. Right sides together and raw edges even, pin and machine-stitch the front to the back around the sides and bottom using a ½-in. seam and pivoting at the bottom corners. Clip into the seam allowances on the curves, snip off the corners of the seam allowances at the bottom, and then press the seam open.

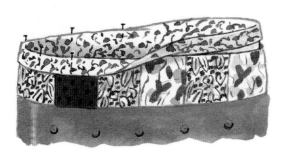

7 Turn under and press a double 1¼-in. hem at the top of the lining. Place the lining, wrong side out, inside the bag, pinning the hem in the lining over the top of the bag. Machine-stitch.

8 For the handles, cut two 3 x 23-in. strips of velvet. Fold one long edge of one strip into the center, wrong sides together, and hand-baste in place. Repeat for the other long edge of the strip. Turn in ¼ in. at each end, and then fold the strip in half lengthwise, enclosing all the raw edges. Pin and machine-stitch along the long edge and both ends. Make the second handle in the same way. Pin one end of each handle to the right side of the front and the other end of each handle to the right side of the back, positioning them evenly. Stitch as shown.

  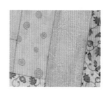

bamboo-handled tote bag

A pair of bamboo handles helps to transform scraps of assorted cotton prints into a pretty tote bag that is a handy enough size to be indispensable on any shopping trip. Inspired by log-cabin patchwork, this design is arranged in a more free and easy way than in the traditional log-cabin pattern. However, the overall effect is the same, with light and dark fabrics positioned diagonally opposite each other for a dramatic contrast.

The bag is 15¼ in. wide x 16 in. high (excluding handles).

You will need:

◆ ⅛ yd. each of cotton fabric in three light prints and three dark prints in shades of the same color, such as pink

◆ Rotary cutter, acrylic ruler, cutting mat (optional)

◆ Matching sewing thread

◆ ⅔ yd. of coordinating fabric, for lining

◆ ½ yd. of fusible interfacing

◆ Paper for pattern

◆ ½ yd. of faux suede in a coordinating color

◆ Pair of 6-in.-wide bamboo handles

◆ Fade-away marker pen

Light and dark shades of one color are often used in log-cabin designs.

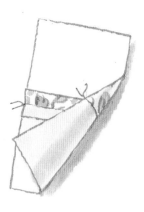

1 This design is made by joining strips to each other, starting with two center squares and working outward using progressively longer strips. Where possible, adjoining strips should be in different prints. From all six fabrics, cut long strips 1¾ in. wide, then cut them to the correct length as you need them. A rotary cutter, acrylic ruler, and cutting mat are more accurate than scissors and will allow you to cut two layers of fabric at a time. Start by cutting out a 1¾-in. square in each of two light fabrics, and pin them right sides together and raw edges even. Machine-stitch a ¼-in. seam. Press the seam open.

2 With the two joined squares arranged one above the other, join a dark strip to the left edge in the same way as in Step 1, trimming off the excess so both ends are even with the top and bottom edges of the two squares, and pressing the seam open. Join a light strip to the bottom of this strip and the adjoining square, again trimming the end so the raw edges are even, and again pressing the seam open.

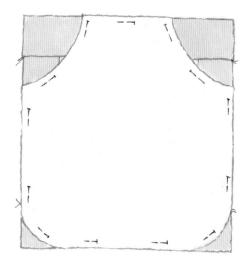

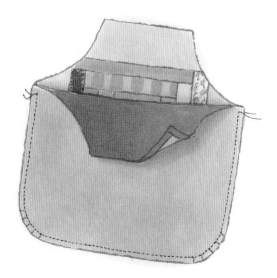

5 Enlarge and transfer the template from page 123 onto paper, then cut out the pattern. Pin the pattern to the patchwork and cut around it. Use the same pattern to cut out two pieces from the lining fabric and one from the faux suede.

6 Pin the patchwork to the faux suede, right sides together and raw edges even, and machine-stitch a ½-in. seam around the bottom and sides, starting and stopping ½ in. from where the bag begins to narrow. Do the same for the two lining pieces. Clip into the seam allowances on the curves at the bottom. Press open the seams. Press under a ½-in. hem along the raw edges of the bag and the lining. Clip into the seam allowances on the top curved edges (being careful not to clip too close to the folds).

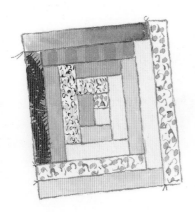

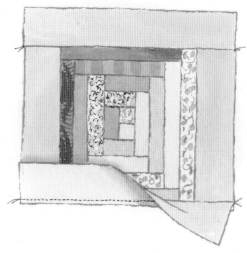

3 Using dark strips on the left side and the top, and light strips on the right side and the bottom, continue piecing in the same way. To create the pattern shown in the photograph, use the following sequence: top, right, top, left, bottom, right, left, top, left, bottom, right, top, bottom, right. Or, for a traditional log-cabin design, always work in the same direction and sequence—right, top, left, bottom, right, top, left, bottom, and so on (counterclockwise).

4 From the lining fabric, cut two strips 2¾-in. wide and as long as the length of the pieced section (about 13 in.). Pin the long edge of one strip to one side edge, right sides together and raw edges even. Machine-stitch a ¼-in. seam, and press the seam open. Join the remaining strip to the other side edge. Now cut two strips 2¾ in. wide and as long as the width of the pieced section (about 16¼ in.), and join these to the top and bottom edges in the same way, to complete the piecing of the front. Cut the interfacing to the same size as the front (about 16¼ x 17½ in.) and, following the manufacturer's instructions, iron it to the wrong side, making sure that the seam allowances are flat.

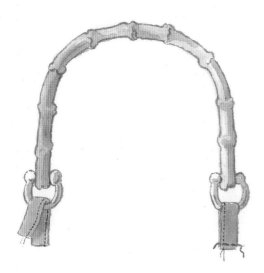

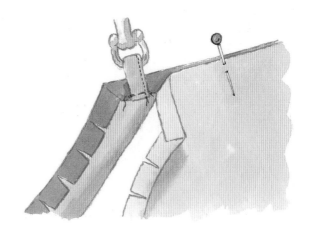

7 Using the bamboo handles as a guide, mark their positions with pins or a chalk pencil on the wrong side of the front and back at the top edges of the bag, an equal distance from each side seam. From one of the prints, cut a 1½ x 8-in. strip. Fold the long raw edges in to meet at the center, press, and then fold in half lengthwise, right side out, and press again. Topstitch close to the edge. Cut it into four equal lengths, and thread these carriers through the rings at the ends of the bamboo handles. Baste the ends of the carriers together. Pin and then baste them to the marked positions on the inside of the bag.

8 Turn the bag right side out. With the lining wrong side out, push it into the bag, matching the side seams. Carefully pin the lining to the bag around the top. Machine-stitch close to the edge, catching in the ends of the carriers at the same time and pivoting at the top corners. Remove the basting.

multicolored tote

Even the slot-handles are part of the pattern of rectangular shapes in this sleek tote. It is made from felted wool, preferably in at least four solid colors for maximum impact. The back is the same as the front, and the two are joined by solid-color sides and a base. Narrow braid, along with some stylized flowers made from the same fabric as the rest of the bag and decorated with seed pearls, provides just enough extra detail to contrast with the right angles of the pattern.

The bag is 13½ in. wide x 17 in. high x 3¼ in. deep.

You will need:

- Paper for patterns
- Scraps of felted wool in at least four shades, such as pink, purple, yellow, and peach
- Rotary cutter, acrylic ruler, cutting mat (optional)
- Matching sewing thread
- Fade-away marker pen and fabric glue

- 6 x 14-in. piece of artist's plastic mesh (available from craft stores)
- 12 seed pearls
- 1 yd. of braid
- ⅔ yd. of fabric, for lining

Soft pastels and simple shapes are combined in this sturdy tote.

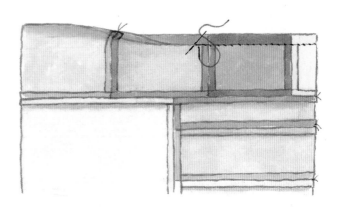

1 Enlarge and transfer the rectangular templates from page 124 onto paper, then cut out the patterns. From your chosen fabrics, cut out two pieces for each rectangular pattern (one of each pair will be used for the back of the bag and the other for the front), making sure that adjacent pieces will be in different colors and the tones will be balanced overall. Also cut out two 4¼ x 18-in. rectangles for the sides and one 4¼ x 14½-in. rectangle for the base, all from one color. A rotary cutter, acrylic ruler, and cutting mat are more accurate than scissors and will allow you to cut two layers of fabric at a time.

2 To piece the front, pin and machine-stitch the pieces, right sides together and raw edges even, using ¼-in. seams and pressing the seams open as you go, in the following sequence. Join the two pieces on the right of the center section, do the same for the four pieces on the left of the center section, and then join these two sections. Join the top four patches into a row, and the bottom two into another row, then join these rows to the top and bottom of the center section. Turn under and press ½ in. along the top edge; hand-sew in place. Make the back in the same way.

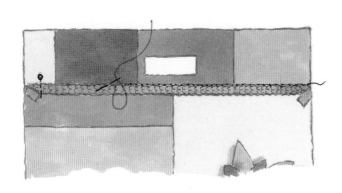

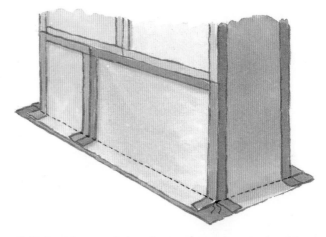

5 Cut a piece of braid the width of the front (about 14½ in.), and hand-sew it to the front along the seamline beneath the handle. Attach braid to the back in the same way. Turn under ½ in. on the top edge of each side piece; press and hand-sew in place.

6 Right sides together and raw edges even, pin the sides to the front along the side edges, and machine-stitch ½-in. seams, leaving the bottom ½ in. of the seams unstitched. Join the remaining side edges of the sides to the back in the same way. Right sides together and raw edges even, pin the base to the bag using ½-in. seams and allowing the unstitched portion of each side seam to open up at each corner, as shown. Adjust the size of the base or the width of the seams, if necessary, for a good fit. Machine-stitch, pivoting at the corners. Snip off the corners of the seam allowances, and press the seams open.

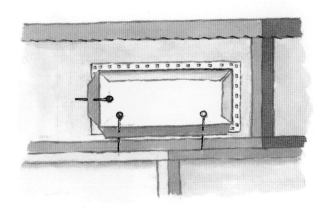

3 On the wrong side of the front, use a fade-away pen to draw a 2¾-in.-long line equal distances from the left and right sides and 1¼ in. from the folded top edge. Draw an identical line 1 in. beneath it, then draw lines joining the ends to form a rectangle; cut this out. From the plastic mesh, cut out a 2 x 3¾-in. rectangle, then cut a 1½ x 3¼-in. rectangular window in it, forming a frame. Place this over the rectangular slot cut in the front, on the wrong side. Clip diagonally into the corners of the fabric as far as the mesh, and fold each edge of the fabric back over the mesh. Pin and hand-sew in place. Make a slot in the back in the same way.

4 Transfer the two flower templates from page 124 onto paper. For the front of the bag, cut out two fabric flowers from each pattern, using a different color for each flower. Repeat to cut out four more flowers for the back. Seal the edges with fabric glue. When dry, sew the four smaller flowers on top of the four larger ones. Embellish each pair with three seed pearls, and hand-sew the flowers to the front and back.

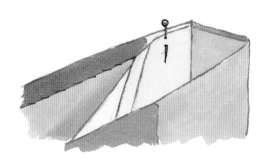

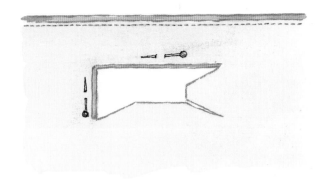

7 Cut a 3¼ x 13½-in. rectangle of plastic mesh (adjusting the size to fit the base if you adjusted that in Step 6). Hand-sew it to the wrong side of the base using a few stitches at each side. Turn the bag right side out. Using the templates, cut out a front, a back, two sides, and a base from the lining fabric. Join these pieces as in Step 6 to form the lining. Press under ⅜ in. at the top of the lining, and then place the lining, wrong side out, inside the bag. The folded top edge of the lining should be ⅛ in. below the folded top edge of the bag. Pin and then machine-stitch through all layers, about ⅛ in. below the folded top edge of the lining.

8 Use a fade-away pen to draw around the slot onto the lining of the front. Draw diagonal lines connecting the corners of the rectangle (forming an X-shape), and cut along these diagonal lines. Fold the resulting triangles to the wrong side of the lining, cut off the points, and slipstitch the lining to the wrong side of the bag around the opening. Repeat for the slot in the back.

diamond-patch tote

Although the front is made up entirely from diamond-shaped pieces of the same size and similar colors, this tote has a rich and sumptuous look. The small scale of the prints and the discreet sparkle of the sequins and tiny beads add just the right amount of delicate detail, while the back is a single piece of luxurious velvet. Be sure to include fabrics in light, medium, and dark tones to create the most pleasing effect.

The bag is 10 in. wide x 15½ in. high (excluding handles).

You will need:

◆ Paper for pattern

◆ Metal ruler and fade-away marker pen

◆ ⅛ yd. each of five print and two solid-color fabrics in coordinating colors, such as blues and greens

◆ Rotary cutter, acrylic ruler, cutting mat (optional)

◆ Matching sewing thread

◆ Set square (optional)

◆ ¼ yd. each of fusible interfacing and lightweight polyester batting

◆ 26 sequins and 26 tiny beads, to match fabric

◆ ⅓ yd. of velvet in coordinating color

◆ ⅓ yd. of fabric in coordinating color, for lining

◆ Pair of 6-in.-wide black handles

Choose small prints in jewel shades for the diamond shapes making up this tote.

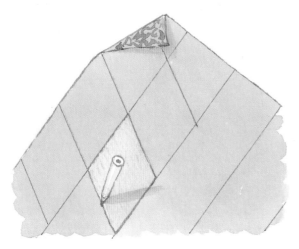

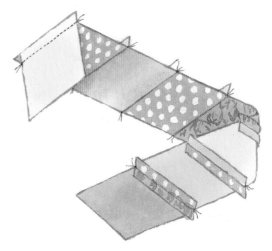

1 Transfer the template from page 125 onto paper, then cut out the pattern. Using a ruler and a fade-away pen or a pencil, mark 2¾-in. strips on one fabric; the total length of the strips will need to be about 33 in. Place the pattern at one end of a strip, aligning two parallel edges of the pattern with those of the strip, and mark the other two sides of one diamond. Move the pattern along and mark more diamonds on the strips until you have nine or ten. Carefully cut out the diamonds. A rotary cutter, acrylic ruler, and cutting mat are more accurate than scissors and will allow you to cut two layers of fabric at a time. Repeat for the remaining fabrics, making 64 diamonds in all.

2 To piece the front, pin one diamond to a second one in a different fabric along one edge, right sides together and raw edges even, and machine-stitch a ¼-in. seam. Repeat to join more diamonds together so that you have a row of eight diamonds. Make seven more rows in the same way. Press open all the seams, and trim off the corners of the seam allowances even with the raw edges. Join the rows to each other in the same way, taking care to match the seamlines.

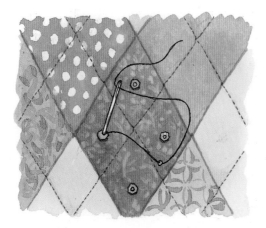

5 Hand-sew sequins with tiny beads in the centers to the diamonds in a symmetrical arrangement, knotting them individually. Cut out a piece of velvet and two pieces of lining, all the same size as the front.

6 Right sides together and raw edges even, pin the patchwork front to the velvet back around the sides and bottom. Machine-stitch a ½-in. seam, pivoting at the bottom corners. Press under a ½-in. seam at the top edges. Snip off the corners of the seam allowances at the bottom, and press open the seams. Trim away the batting within the seam allowance. Press. Make the lining in the same way.

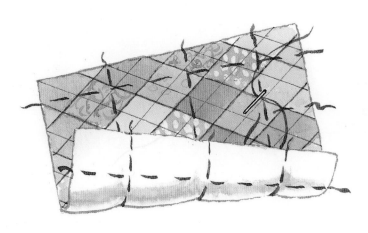

3 Turn the front as shown and use a ruler and a fade-away pen or a chalk pencil to draw a rectangle on it, with the points on the edges of the front. Use a set square or the corner of a piece of paper to make sure the corners of the rectangle are square. The rectangle will be about 11 x 16½ in. Carefully cut out the front along the drawn lines. Cut out a piece of interfacing and a piece of batting to the same size. Following the manufacturer's instructions, iron the interfacing to the wrong side of the patchwork, making sure that the seam allowances are flat.

4 On the right side of the front, use a fade-away pen and ruler to draw a grid of straight lines running through the center of each diamond, parallel to the sides of the diamonds. Pin the batting to the wrong side of the front, and hand-baste it in place using large running stitches from top to bottom, side to side, and corner to corner. Remove the pins. Now machine-stitch along the marked lines, starting from the center and working outward. Remove the basting.

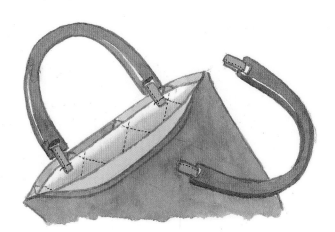

7 Using the black handles as a guide, mark their position with pins or the fade-away pen on the wrong side of the front and back at the top edges of the bag, equal distances from each side seam. From one of the prints, cut a 1½ x 8-in. strip. Fold the long raw edges in to meet at the center, press, and then fold in half lengthwise, right side out, and press again. Topstitch close to the edge. Cut it into four equal lengths, and thread these carriers through the holes at the ends of the black handles. Baste the ends of the carriers together. Pin and then baste them to the marked positions on the inside of the bag.

8 Turn the bag right side out. With the lining wrong side out, push it into the bag, matching the side seams. Carefully pin the top edge of the lining about ⅛ in. below the top of the bag. Machine-stitch close to the edge, catching in the ends of the carriers at the same time. Remove the basting.

 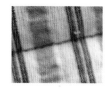 

girl's overnight tote

Any young girl will find this tote bag irresistible, whether for carrying pajamas to a sleepover or for storing treasures at home. Large plastic handles and a boxy shape make it very practical and roomy as well as versatile. The focus of the design, both front and back, is the fun novelty fabric used for six big patches, framed by solid-colored and striped fabric strips that are quick and easy to sew together.

 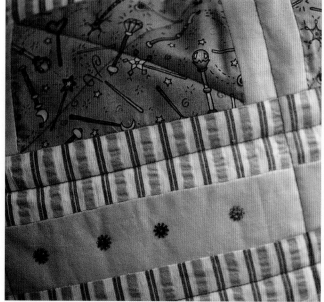

The bag is 15 in. wide x 16 in. high (excluding handles) x 2½ in. deep.

You will need:

◆ ⅓ yd. each of a novelty fabric, a solid-color fabric, and a striped fabric

◆ Rotary cutter, acrylic ruler, cutting mat (optional)

◆ Matching sewing thread

◆ 24 sequins

◆ ½ yd. of fusible interfacing

◆ ½ yd. of lightweight polyester batting

◆ Fade-away marker pen

◆ ⅔ yd. of muslin

◆ 3 x 15-in. piece of artist's plastic mesh (available from craft stores)

◆ Pair of 6-in.-wide clear plastic handles

Choose soft pastels or bright primary colors for this fun and modern tote.

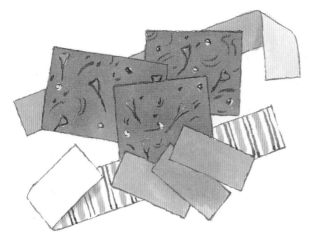

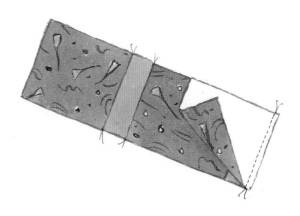

1 From the novelty fabric, cut out strips 3¾ in. wide and totaling at least 58 in. in length. Cut the strips into eight rectangles 4½ in. long and four rectangles 5½ in. long. From the solid-color fabric, cut out a 1¾ x 30-in. strip, and cut it into eight pieces 3¾ in. long. Also from this fabric, cut out two 2 x 16-in. strips and four 1¾ x 16-in. strips. From the striped fabric, cut out eight 2 x 16-in. strips. A rotary cutter, acrylic ruler, and cutting mat are more accurate than scissors and will allow you to cut two layers of fabric at a time.

2 Right sides together, raw edges even, and using ¼-in. seams, pin and machine-stitch the long edges of two short solid-color strips to the short edges of three novelty-fabric pieces. A narrower rectangle should be on each side and a wider one in the middle, separated by the solid-color strips. Press the seams open. Make three more pieced rows in the same way.

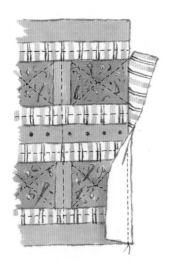

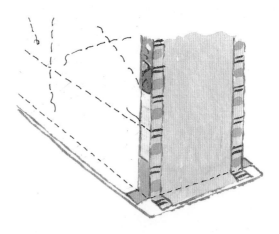

5 From the striped fabric, cut two 3½ x 14½-in. strips for the sides, and one 3½ x 16-in. strip for the base. Right sides together and raw edges even, pin the sides to the front along the side edges, with the top edge of each side extending ½ in. above the top seamline of the novelty-fabric pieces. Machine-stitch ½-in. seams, leaving the top and bottom ½ in. of the seams unstitched. Join the remaining side edges of the sides to the back in the same way. Press under ½ in. on the top edge of the front, sides, and back. Clip into the seam allowance of the bag side edge at the top of each side piece, and press under the seam allowance.

6 Right sides together and raw edges even, pin the base to the bag using ½-in. seams and allowing the unstitched portion of each side seam to open up at each corner, as shown. Adjust the size of the base or the width of the seams, if necessary, for a good fit. Machine-stitch, pivoting at the corners. Snip off the corners of the seam allowances, press the seams open, and trim away the batting within the seam allowance. Press under a ½-in. hem along the top raw edges. For the lining front and back, cut out two 16 x 17-in. rectangles from the muslin, along with the same strips as for the bag sides and base. (See Step 5.) Then make the lining as in Steps 5 and 6.

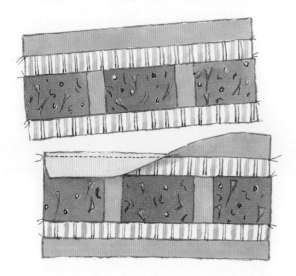

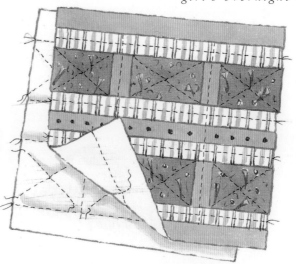

3 In the same way, join a striped strip to the top of each pieced row, and another to the bottom. Join a narrow solid-color strip to the top of one pieced section, and another to the bottom of another pieced section. Now join a wider solid-color strip to the other edge of each of these two pieced sections, so they are all joined, forming the front. Repeat with the remaining strips and pieced rows to make the back. Hand-sew sequins along the center of the middle strip on the front and back. Cut out two pieces each of interfacing and batting, to the size of the front and back (about 16 x 17 in.). Following the manufacturer's instructions, iron the interfacing to the wrong side of the front and back, making sure that the seam allowances are flat.

4 On the right side of the front and back, use a fade-away pen and ruler to draw a straight line running through the center of each striped strip. Also draw vertical lines running through the center of each vertical solid-color strip, from the top striped strip to the bottom striped strip, and draw diagonal lines from corner to corner of each of the novelty-fabric rectangles. Pin the pieces of batting to the wrong side of the front and back, and hand-baste in place using large running stitches from top to bottom, side to side, and corner to corner. Remove the pins. Now machine-stitch along the marked lines, starting from the center and working outward. Remove the basting.

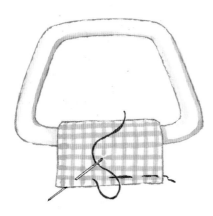

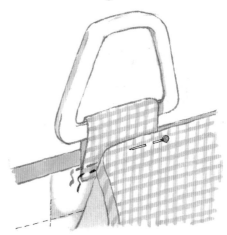

7 Cut a 2½ x 15-in. rectangle of plastic mesh (adjusting the size to fit the base if you adjusted that in Step 6). Hand-sew it to the wrong side of the base using a few stitches at each side. For the two carriers, cut two 3½ x 9-in. rectangles from the muslin. Fold one in half crosswise, right sides together. Machine-stitch a ¼-in. seam down the short edge. Press the seam open, turn right side out, and press again. Repeat for the other rectangle. Wrap each carrier around a handle, and baste the raw edges together at the end, then baste the ends of one carrier in the center of the top edge on the wrong side of the front, and the ends of the other in the same position on the wrong side of the back.

8 Turn the bag right side out and press. With the lining wrong side out, push it into the bag, matching the side seams. Carefully pin the lining to the bag around the top. Machine-stitch close to the edge, catching in the ends of the handles at the same time. Remove the basting.

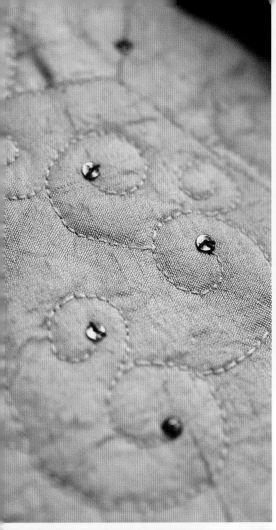

gift bags

A handmade gift is always special, reflecting the time, effort, and skill you've put into making it. A patchwork bag will be particularly welcome because it is so useful. It is the perfect present, since you can personalize it according to the tastes, interests, and lifestyle of the recipient. By choosing the fabrics and trimmings carefully, you can even make it appropriate to the birthday, anniversary, holiday, or other occasion on which you are giving it. Any one of the bags included in this chapter would make a delightful gift, although once you have made it, you may decide that you simply cannot part with it.

wooden-handled bag

Taking its inspiration from a traditional knitting bag, this charming patchwork bag is a great way to make the most of pretty scraps that might have gone unused otherwise. A versatile size, it will make a popular gift. It could be used for a variety of purposes, such as a carryall for needlecraft materials or as a summer bag. At the top, where the patchwork wraps around the curved handles, the bag has a softly gathered look that contrasts well with the chunky wood. Bright rickrack and buttons add to the colorful effect.

The bag is 21 in. wide x 13 in. high (excluding handles).

You will need:

◆ Scraps of about five print fabrics

◆ Rotary cutter, acrylic ruler, cutting mat (optional)

◆ Matching sewing thread

◆ 1 yd. of rickrack in first color, such as green

◆ 1⅔ yd. of rickrack in second color, such as pink

◆ 25 assorted buttons

◆ Pair of 6-in.-wide round wooden handles

This bright carryall is a witty twist on grandma's knitting bag.